Nameless

by Charles Buckley

Savage
PRESS
Box 115, Superior, WI 54880 (715) 394-9513

First Edition

ISBN 1-886028-04-4

Library of Congress Catalog Card Number: 00-100208

Published by:

Savage Press
P.O. Box 115
Superior, WI 54880

715-394-9513

e-mail: savpress@spacestar.com

Visit us at: www.savpress.com

Printed in the USA

Table of Contents

Introduction

This is the author's fourth book. Charles Buckley has also written <u>North of Sixty</u>, <u>Don't Cry For Me</u> and <u>Polar Verse</u>. Those books were primarily about life in the Arctic and Sub-Arctic. This book, though it contains some work with an Arctic setting and also some work found in previous works, is of broader spectrum. Since it covers many different settings and different views, the book is entitled "Nameless".

The author is an American but also has an affinity to Canada, the Canadian Arctic and the city of Montreal to which he has returned many times and continues to. He has also traveled over the United States, Great Britain, France, Mexico, the Carribean, Alaska and Siberia in the former Soviet Union. He presently lives in Superior, Wisconsin USA and is the president and founder of Century Insurance Agency, Inc. Mr. Buckley attended the University of Minnesota, served in the American Navy and worked as a Claims Examiner for the American government before entering the insurance field.

Foreword

If I upon a looser creed
Have strung the jewel of good deed
Let that for my atonement plead.
Often, one for two did I misread
But now for much of what I am
Thanks must go to Omar Khayyám

Along with thanks to Rudyard Kipling,
Robert Burns and Robert W. Service.

Omar put his thoughts in ink
Long before the later three
But all those four made me think
And helped to set my mind free

Of much prejudice, superstition and
other garbage.

*Any characters depicted in the poems are fictional and
are not to be confused with anyone living or dead.*

-Author

Forethought

Since some of the material in this book are quotations from works of Robert Burns, Rudyard Kipling, Omar Khayyam and Robert W. Service, the author thinks it appropriate to give short resumes on these poets. Therefore, the following is presented.

Robert Burns was a Scottish poet born in 1759 and died in 1796. His works have become well known over most of the world. Some of his best known poems are A Red Rose, "Auld Lang Syne" and "Comin' Thro' the Rye."

Omar Khayyám was born in 1048 and died in 1122 (nearly a thousand years ago). He was a Persian mathmetician, astronomer and philosopher, and was not known as a poet in his lifetime. In 1959 Edward Fitzgerald, a well known English country gentlemen, translated a selection of Khayyám's poetry which is largely skeptical and hedonistic in nature.

Rudyard Kipling was born in 1856 and died in 1936. He was a British poet born in England, spent time in India and a great amount of his work had an Indian setting. He was a great supporter of the British Empire and the British Commonwealth. He also wrote some children's stories and his works are known world wide.

Robert W. Service was born in 1874 and died in 1958. He was of Scots origin, born in England, came to Canada in 1894, worked in the bank at Whitehorse, Yukon Territory. He was fascinated by the Canadian Yukon and the strangeness of the Arctic. Most of his work has an Arctic flavor. He is particularly well known for his works of the Yukon (Canadian). His works are even much admired by the people of Alaska and, even though he was not an American, he might also be considered to be one of the favorites, if not the favorite poet of Alaska. Two of his favorite poems are Spell Of The Yukon and The Cremation of Sam McGee.

Moose stands by cow

In Shrewsbury, Vermont, a few years back, a lovesick moose wondered onto the farm of Larry Carrara and fell in love with Jessica. It was moose mating season and the gigantic forest denizen could not stop mooning over poor Jessica. The love was unrequited, as Jessica was a brown and White Hereford cow.

The cold shoulder from Jessica didn't seem to discourage the moose. He hung around Carrara's heard for over 40 days, eating apple tree twigs and shoving other cows away from grain so Jessica could eat more.

Moose experts said it was impossible for an offspring to result from this amoré, but that mooses falling in love with horses has been well documented. The experts said that the moose would return to the forest when mating season ended.

While the moose stood by his cow, the world watched via TV and listening to the radio reports. Over 60,000 people drove by the Carrara Farm to observe the inter-species love. All the hoopla eventually settled down. The moose went away. Jessica mooed and the crowds vanished.

What remained was a lesson in love that impressed people worldwide.

- From News Reports

Nameless

Grass Over Love

There was a big bull moose
From the state of Vermont
Who fell head over hoofs
For a cow named LaMont.

She rejected his advances
And refused him a date
She ignored his amorous glances,
And tagged him second rate.

He could not understand
And thought that she was crass,
Yea, sadly, he was right
All she wanted was some grass.

She then put her hoof down
With a warning, straight out,
"It's not love, but good grass
That's my life's all about.

"You may think as you wish
And all this and all that;
The love bug has got you,
But, to me, it's old hat.

"I'm supplied all my grass
By a farmer each day;
You must forage for yours.
For me, that's no way.

"So forget it 'Old Moose,'
You are Moosedom's Clark Gable;
But I'll keep my farmer
Who puts grass on my table."

Nameless

Inside
Out

The Man In The Glass

When you get lost in your struggles for self
And the world makes you king for a day,
Just go to a mirror and look at yourself
And see what THAT man has to say.

For it isn't your father or mother or wife
Who judgement upon you must pass
The fellow whose verdict counts most in your life
Is the one staring back from the glass.

Some people may think you a straight shooting chum
And call you a wonderful guy
But the man in the glass says you're only a bum
If you can't look him straight in the eye.

He's the fellow to please, never mind all the rest
For he's with you clear up to the end
And you've passed your most dangerous difficult test
If the man in the glass is your friend.

You may fool the whole world down the pathway of life
And get pats on your back as you pass
But your final reward will be heartaches and tears
If you cheat the man in the glass.

Make me thoughtful, not moody, helpful, but not bossy. Release me from the craving to try to straighten out everybody's affairs. Teach me the glorious lesson that occasionally I may be mistaken (Excerpt from The Nun's Poem.)

Aggressive acts are merely the sign of a sick soul.

Don't be angry that you cannot change others as you wish them to be, as it is sometimes very difficult to change yourself to what you might wish to be. - Thomas à Kempis - Christian Philosopher.

A Time To Change Course

Are we a nation gone to pot
Where children carry handguns
And the passerby is shot?
Do our leaders "pull the wool"
As our cities burn and rot?
They use *our* money as if it were their's
And then say, "Forget Me Not."

We seek some relaxation
At the local "Movie Palace."
We hear verbs of sex — a fixation,
See acts of bloody violence;
Instead of scenes of inspiration.
Are they "movies" or just junk
That demand our condemnation?

Lordy, Lordy why are we now
In this big puddle of mud
Of what was a shining sea?
Lying is just, "one of those things,"
With TRUTH no where to see.
We can't blame him or her
It's we and only you and me.

It is WE who must change course;
A time for action – not remorse.

Indian Influence On English

Shown below are a few of the many English words brought into common usage by the British which derive from Indian languages.

Bungalow: A type of one story dwelling with a veranda was first built in India. The word derives from the Hindi bangla meaning "belonging to Bengal."

Dungarees: The course fabric worn by poorer Indians — dungri in Hindi.

Nabob: A nawab in Hindustani was a provincial governor, hence a special personage.

Paraih: The word for outcast comes from the Tamil paralyan, a member of a low Hindu caste.

Punch: The five part mixture of alcohol, water, sugar, lemon and spice gets it's name from the Hindu word for five-panch.

Shampoo: The massage described by European travelers in India in the 17th century was called in Hindustani, champo.

Thug: A member of a northern religious sect espousing murder was called in Hindustani, a thag. The sect was suppressed by the British.

Footnote:
This page is dedicated to my doctor and long time dear friend, Dr. Kevin Ramesh who was born in India and passed away in July 1999. The author in his personal friendship with Dr. Ramesh learned much, as did the British from the Indian People. Dr. Ramesh belonged to the profession which the great poet Rudyard Kipling says the following in this poem:

Doctors: He was of the bold, seekers of the way —
        The passionless, the unshakable of the soul,
        Who serve the inmost mysteries of man's clay
        And ask no more than leave to make them whole.

Prayer of St. Francis of Assisi

LORD

Make me an instrument
of Your peace;
Where there is hatred, let me sow love;
Where there is injury, pardon;
Where there is doubt, faith;
Where there is despair, hope;
Where there is darkness, light;
Where there is sadness, joy.

O DIVINE MASTER

Grant that I may not so much
seek to be consoled as to console;
To be understood as to understand;
To be loved as to love.

For it is in giving that we receive.
It is in pardoning that
we are pardoned.
It is in dying that we
are born to eternal life.

St. Francis of Assisi — A Christian Saint.

Fireweed in the Yukon

There's a fireweed up in the Yukon
That I am going back to see
She may be way up in the Dawson
Or by the far-off Beaufort Sea.

Fireweed is the flower of Yukon
And abundant in that northern place
But the flower that I refer to
Is just a girl of native race,

I was young and she was younger
And as such knew not my mind
Like the man who always sightless
Could not see that he was blind.

Grass looks green on the other side
That is why the cow jumps the fence
So I goodbyed and left the scene
Now it's time to do my penance.

I left the quiet and pristine
To taste of the big city life
'Twasn't long until I had my fill
That was no place to find a wife.

I found I had it good and blew it
And of leaving, I now reflect
That I was dumb as dumb can be
I even bow and genuflect.

I can see her in her parka
Feeding and caring for her dogs
Or stirring coals in the campfire
And later throwing in some logs.

No Racism

A great white raven
Left his old haven
To lead a new life
And find a black wife.

There was no applause
As he flaunted the laws
That ravens should heed,
"Black with black must breed."

Whitey pitched his woo
To a bird name Sue
He wasted no time;
Wedding bells did chime.

"No stones or sticks
Black with white may mix
Down with old laws of hate
Let's get up to date."

The priest went on to say,
"I bid you this day
Believe and be grateful
That white is beautiful."

Now at the Flyers Club
The Whiteys come for some grub.
One can hear the gossipy clack,
"Those kids, half white and half black!"

The Robin and The Cross

The road there is quite narrow;
Autos few and spaced far apart.
Beside is a small pile of dirt
It's something to tear at your heart.

On top of that small heap of earth
There stands a small white cross
A symbol to remind us always
Of much suffering and loss.

The body is not that of us humans
That is buried to become clay
But the remains of a small robin
That already had seen its last day.

The robin was crossing the road
Returning to its mama's nest
When out of the blue came an auto,
Without stopping, broke the bird's breast.

Next upon the scene, a passerby
Who took the little body aside
Caressing the feathers gently
While carrying it on its "last ride."

Next came the movement of hands
In the work of movement of ground
And then the planting of the cross
At the top of the mound.

We don't see mockery of any faith
But rather the absence of joy
The grave maker and cross builder
Was just a small boy.

He truly loved robins
And was a Christian.

The Putdown

There was a mighty St. Bernard
Who fell in love with a lioness.
He pursued her with much gusto;
Treated her with full finesse.

His heart put him in high gear;
Puppy love had him by the paw.
He was blind to her feelings
And of his flaunting natural law.

Finally she thrust her claws out
Saying, "This must come to a stop,
You are just a big ugly mutt
Get going or I'll blow my top.

"Let me tell you straight out
There is another big hitch,
My dad is king of the jungle
You are just a son of a bitch."

20

A Pet Cat

We see the cat
Crippled by love
Her claws are gone
Defenseless from now on.

Treated as a child
But not far from wild
A substitute for motherhood
A solace to widowhood.

Place Love

It's up there in the NWT
That still claims part of me
No matter where I do roam
Home will always be
Away up north in the NWT.

Footnote: NWT — Northwest Territories, CANADA:
It is as big as Alaska, Texas, California
and two other states of the U.S., extends into the
Arctic and has only about 50,000 people, mostly
Innuit (Eskimo).

Nameless

Passages

Wisdom?

The Vampire*

A fool there was and he made his prayer
(Even as you and I)
To a rag and a bone and a hank of hair
(We called her the woman who didn't care)
But the fool he called her his lady fair . . .
(Even as you and I)

Oh, the years we waste and the tears we waste
And the work of our head and hand
Belong to the woman who did not know
(And now we know that she never could know)
And did not understand!

The fool was stripped to his foolish hide
(Even as you and I)
Which she might have seen when she threw him aside —
(But isn't it on record the lady tried?)
So some of him lived, but most of him died . . .
(Even as you and I)

And it isn't the shame and it isn't the blame
That stings like a white hot brand . . .
It's coming to know that she could never know why.
(Seeing at last that she could never know why)
And never could understand.

From the verse by the same name by the great British author and poet Rudyard Kipling.

Mistakes are merely steps in the ladder of success.
— *Robert W. Service, Canadian Poet*

24

Parka Wedding

They were of God's frozen people
And away from church or steeple
But honest was the pact they made
Without fanfare or serenade.

Strange to us were that native pair
In wedding, their perils to share
As the symbol, traded some fur
Without a priest or barrister.

Token of sharing the same home
Till Hell froze on the arctic dome
Was exchange of garments both wore
On the way to Eternity's shore.

It was their parkas they did trade
Signs of union of man with maid;
Best of all the contract did last,
They clung to each other steadfast.

Their needs were few, their wants the same
Joint survival, their only aim
He to feed them, such was the case
She to cook, sew and bear the race.

We with all our ceremony
In holy acts of matrimony
Could learn from them, simple they were
And their pact with a piece of fur.

Right it is that we pledge our troth
Before judge or man of the cloth
That is our law and tradition
But what counts is our intentions.

New Trinity

There was a priest in the taiga
Who thought God was a chaika
But he stuck to the trinity
That to him was divinity
So when he did genuflect
He took care to reflect,
"In the name of the Father, the Son
and the Chaika."

Footnote — Taiga: Russian swampland
Chaika: seagull
Priest: Russian Orthodox

The Rubáiyát

Wake for the sun who scattered in to flight
The stars before him from a field of night
Drive night along with them from Heaven and strikes
The sultan's turret with a shaft of light.

Before the phantom of false morning died
When all the temple is prepared within
Why nods the drowsy worshipper outside?

And as the cock crew those who stood before
The tavern shouted, "Open then the door!
You know how little time we have to stay
And once departed may return no more."

You rising moon that looks for us again
How oft hereafter look for us?
How oft hereafter will she wax and wane
Thru this same garden and for one in vain?

And when like her, O Saki you shall pass
Among the guest stars seated on the grass
And in your joyous errand reach the spot
Where I made one turn down an empty glass.

—*Omar Khayyám*

The exalted shall be humbled
and the humble shall be exalted

The Bible.

Instead of the Bible being looked upon as "divine truth" it
should be looked upon as a record of the barbarous acts
of long ago when the human race was groping for a path
of light in the darkness of ignorance, superstition and
slavery. When we look upon it from that aspect, we can
learn much as there is as much wisdom in it as there is in
the Koran and books of like nature.

Wisdom?

O wad some Power the giftie gie us
To see ourselves as others see us!
It wad frae monie a blunder free us,
an' foolish notion:
What airs in dress and gait wad lea'e us
An ev'n devotion

Robert Burns

Whenever the Lord builds a house of prayer
The Devil builds a chapel there
And it's found upon investigation
That the Devil has the largest congregation.

Anonymous

Selfishness

Death takes our loved ones . . .
We are bowed in grief. For whom?
Are we not selfish?
A mourner weeps for himself,
The dead know not of sorrow.

If a body meet a body
    Coming through the rye
If a body kiss a body
    need a body cry?
If a body meet a body
Coming through the glen
If a body kiss a body
Need the whole world ken?*

Robert Burns

*ken is Scottish for English know.

Wisdom?

Come fill the cup and in the fire of spring
Your winter garment of repentance fling;
The bird of time has but little way to flutter
And the bird is on the wing.

A book of verses underneath the bough
A jug of wine, a loaf of bread — and thou
Beside me singing in the wilderness . . .
And wilderness is Paradise now.

Omar Khayyám

Nameless

Etc...

Ode to a Bat

Like leaves in trees they hang suspended
Waiting for the night to fall
And as day is finally ended
Taking flight, they heed the call.

As evening darkness dims the light
And slowly daytime turns to night
The swooping bats will break their fast
As airborne insects they quickly grasp

Shadowy silhouettes blurred with speed
Hungrily fulfill their need
Threading an unerring path
Through a maze of branches filigreed.

If speed a measure of intelligence be
Then even scoffers may agree
That bats may sometimes outwit men
With wondrous skill beyond the ken.

Donald E. Jonasson, Lancaster, Ontario, Canada

34

PIIA

How can I describe her?
Words can find a way;
Daughter of Light and Innocence
Half child and half woman.

Yet there is truth in her,
And if there is beauty in truth
Then she is truly beautiful
A soul unspoiled by greed.

An Eden on the edge of Hell
To know her is to love her
Therefore I fear to know her,
Yet she must be loved.

So be it, that her image will not die
But be rekindled to provide
That hope for jaded beings
Such as I.

Donald E. Jonasson, Lancaster, Ontario, Canada

Columbus Day*...
or
A Helping Hand

This is an Indian view
Of the voyage of ninety two
And the events that came
With the Columbus claim.

The world became much smaller;
Spain's gold heap grew taller.
It stole land from the Red,
Left many an Indian dead.

Our Gods did not suffice
As we became the sacrifice
We had our Chief Crazy Horse
But white chiefs were worse.

To each his own, so they say —
We, as victims rue the day
When the Gringos took our land;
They called it a helping hand.

550th anniversary of Columbus discovery

A Gopher is
A Gopher

This tale is of Gus from Swedetown
A little town in Minnesota
For his honesty he was renown;
For the fast lane cared not one iota.

Gopher state was all that he knew
May not have been an intellect;
Knew all that Luther said was true,
Spoke English with a dialect.

Came the war with a stint in D.C.
Right close by the Capitol Dome.
An unhappy clodhopper was he
Miles and miles away from home.

Here was the big city with its zoom
Also with its rot and its roar
Exhaust smells instead of legume
City life to Gus was a bore.

The war ended as all wars do
With time for a new start.
When asked what he would pursue
Came his reply as he rushed to depart.

"I have had enough of D.C. primates
And other things, my full quota
I am leaving the United States
And going back to Minnesota."

Footnote — Gopher: Nickname for a resident of Minnesota

A Letter To A Departed Loved One

This letter is late
To an unknown shore
Most of it not new
But just a bit more.

Death stalks around us
Most of it we ignore
The pain comes when it
Arrives at our door.

The stalker has come
And now you are gone
Our green grass of life
Is now a scorched lawn.

It wasn't all roses
We all share some strife
But something kept us
Together in life.

Time moves on quickly
And softens the sting
Our own end will come
That time too will bring.

Then some will read this
But only by chance
They won't understand
Just give it a glance.

We cannot blame them
'Twas not their affair
Our loss is because
Of the life we did share.

This note cannot end
With the usual adieu
All that we can say is
We miss you, we miss you, we miss you.

Smart Monkey

"This is a just war"
That is what we say
If we don't win it
It will be hell to pay.

Labels won't change it
We know we must win
But also know that all wars
Are brought on by men.

Call it as you wish,
It's a bloody business
It's an affliction,
A form of madness.

War has been with us
Since Adam or before.
When will be rid of
All the blood and gore?

The Ape sits in his tree
Telling his dependents
How much smarter they are
Than their descendants,

"We may kill our kind
For food or a mate
But to kill in war groups
In that we hesitate.

40

"We look at Man's wars
And feel quite spunky.
Are we ever so glad
To still be a monkey!"

Footnote — Man may be the only member of its species that kills its own kind in group wars.

The Church Bike Excursion

We pedal, pedal, pedal,
And ride merrily along.
The Good Book is in our grasp,
And we sing a Godly song.

We have our morning lesson,
But have no wine in our cup.
A bit of grape will help
To keep us on the up and up.

Up, up o'er the hills of life
We avoid the sinful edge;
Tracking the straight and narrow
With love to our Savior pledge.

This is our yearly bike trip;
One more part of life to run.
Boys and girls and preacher man;
God be with us, it is fun.

It's He who gives us strength
As we read His Holy word
He will bring us back safely
As we travel for our Lord.

It's Not Easy

to apologize
to begin over
to take advice
to admit error
to be charitable
to keep on trying
to be considerate
to profit by mistakes
to forgive and forget
to think and then act
BUT IT ALWAYS PAYS OFF

Mud thrown is ground lost

Nameless

Dead Heat

A Male Chauvinist View of a Beargrease Race

The track was rough
The men were tough
The race was on
From dusk to dawn

The end had come
On this dog run
Then came the test
A woman was best

How did men flop
With a woman on top?
Man should be best
And lead the rest.

From an old sourdough
These words of woe,
"Not she who done it.
It was the dogs who won it."

Footnote — Sourdough: One who has lived through 4 seasons in the North.

Drive Carefully

Here lies the body of Emily White
Signaled left, then turned right.

Beneath this slab
Hand Sark is stowed
Watched the girls
And not the road

When behind the wheel
Drive with care.
Drive like Hell,
And you may soon get there.

Auto vs. Gun

Hurray, Hurray, we are alive
The car was dead on arrival
After a collision at fifty-five.

Were we travelling too fast?
Was it the work of God or Allah
That we are present, not past?

No matter, time marches on
Here in the land of the living
Our presence our only Icon.

This has taught us a lesson,
An auto can be as dangerous
As a Smith & Wesson.

The Best Discovery

There are those who say the lever
Was the best dicovery ever
There are those who will say the wheel
Is best of all, the biggest deal.

Yes, both put man in the fast lane
Gave him some tools for greater gain
But they must come out second best
As there is one who tops the rest.

I say man gained the biggest wad
The day that he discovered God
And His commandments not to sin
That could be used as tools on men,

Wheel and lever used by man
To run machines from fan to van
But God even ranked above gold
His uses were more manifold.

He could make the mighty cower
Bring sunshine to the darkest hour
Make castor oil taste like honey
Even aid in getting money.

Whether you believe or reflect
We judge here of use and effect
We look not to color or size
Overall useage takes the prize.

In discovery or invention
God is winner, my contention.

Nameless

P.S.

Two Old Friends

Just a kiss or maybe two
At the time of departure
More of a friendly good-bye
Than full of youthful rapture
With these two old friends.

He had no designs on her
Except that friendship must stay
Passions of love had to be
Consigned to a former day
With these two old friends.

They knew from the past that life
Is subject to fickle fate
That every moment must count
As it was already quite late
With these two old friends.

Oh, life is like a snow trail
With many a slippery slope.
But the real bottom line
Is happiness funded by hope.
Even among two old friends.

Song of Alaska

Eight stars of gold on a field of blue
Alaska's flag. May it mean to you,
The blue of the sea, the evening sky
The mountain lakes and the flowers nearby
The gold of the early sourdough's dreams.
The precious gold of the hills and streams,
The brilliant stars in the northern sky
The "Bear" — the "Dipper" and shining high,
The great North Star with its steady light
Over the land and sea, a beacon bright.
Alaska's flag to Alaskans dear,
The simple flag of a last frontier.

A Neater Sweeter Maiden

There in a wind swept igloo
Far north by the Bering Sea
Lives a tiny Innuit lady.
I hope she will wait for me.

The first time that I saw her
She was rocking to and fro
In her geeing and her hawing
The sled dogs in the snow.

Her feet were tightly bound
In mukluks of reindeer hide
Her figure, God's great gift
To escape from infanticide.

Beneath the aurora borealis
She welcomed my embrace
With no thoughts of conflict
Between white and native race.

To latch on to her — not my fate
I goodbyed and went my way
With mountains as a backdrop
Fronted by an icy bay.

Now my heart is longing
For that lovely Innuit
I am going north and ask her
To make my life complete

"Oh my love will you be mine?"
Those words to her I will say;
Then I hope she will answer,
"Yes, Dear, forever and a day."

Some may think me bonkers,
I know they won't understand
That I found a neater sweeter maiden
In a cleaner, whiter, colder land.

Footnotes — Geeing: Asking the dogs to go left
Hawing: Asking the dogs to go right
Innuit: Native word for Eskimo
Bonkers: Slang for "crazy"
Infanticide: The killing of babies

Goodbye to Painting

He was not a Toulouse Lautrec
But did have a problem with paint
It was paint that made a wreck
Of his love life and his complaint

It was not to just dabble a brush
That brought on his trouble
And put the last touch on his crush;
More than that to blow up Love's bubble.

Her castle needed a face lift;
Pronto, a paint brush was in his hand
With, "Love is not a free gift,
Use that brush that's in your hand."

Her home was a storied affair
Requiring platform and ladder
As he painted up there in the air
He became madder and madder.

SHE kept his nose to the grindstone
Many times he felt like fainting;
He was tired in muscle and bone,
But the order, "keep on painting."

When one's feet are held to the fire
Time limits are set by the heat
He soon knew that this love must expire
And the time had come to retreat.

Later thoughts of women came up
All mixed up with house paint.
"You sure have had your full cup,
Go some place where paint, there aint."

North he went to the Beaufort Sea
To the cold land of the Innuit
Latched on to Tukturjuit Annie
Who thought man was a "treat."

We know that igloos need no paint,
She is happy with her brown face.
From him you will hear no complaint
In that cold, cold empty space.

He is happy on his big pile of ice
And his Ex can paint her own hutch
To him life is tranquil and nice
Attended to by his Yukonese Clutch.

Footnotes — *Tukturjuit: Caribou*
Clutch: Yukon term for woman or wife
Innuit: Native word for Eskimo

My Trinity

There are many with money debt
But such is not the case with me
I'm free of money bills, but yet
Owing much to a trinity.

Oh, the debt is very real
But of a kind that makes me free
A string that keeps me taut with zeal
Yet fills my life with harmony.

Not with any sum of money
That big, big bill can I repay
What's more it isn't even funny
The debt gets bigger every day.

The debt is not signed for nor sealed
This trinity is not for all
It is their wisdom that revealed
To me much of our greed and fall.

This trinity helped us to think;
To think is the greatest gift to man
Their gift is putting their thoughts in ink
That differs us from the orang-utan.

To everyone, their own divinity
Whatever turns your crank
Whatever gives of serenity
And choose which God you wish to thank.

My trinity were three plain men
Just poets from whom we can learn
To heed them not would by my sin
Kipling, Service and Burns.

With the three let's choose a Godhead
Different from another clan
A wise poet of 1000 year dead
Master of Wisdom — Omar Khayyám.

The Monica Song

There is a Mr. Big-Big in D.C.
The son of a gun didn't use a gun
But he made a wounded woman out of me.

Did he lull me in to La-La land
Or did I do some lulling too?
Lordy-Lordy, take my hand.

Grass is green on the other side
That is why the bull jumps the fence
Mr. Big-Big ranges far and wide.

Friends say, "He would not hurt a flea."
Many others just do not care
But he made a wounded woman out of me.

No gun or knife was there to see
But just the same, Big-Big's game
Made a wounded woman out of me.

Going West

The skyline of Toronto
Is great to look on to,
But we're going past it.

Somewhere else does call
Goodbye too to Montreal
It's "Westward Ho" for us.

We'll throw the old beret
It's not the western way
And a chapeau won't do.

We'll buy a cowboy hat
No need for a cravat
Out in the prairies.

Lets forget Molson too
Quaff some mountain dew
Looking at the Rodeo.

We'll gawk at the Stampede
Smell some tumbleweed
Way out there in the West

We won't give a care
About what duds we wear
Just some casual garb

Out there in that big, big land
There is no speech with forked tongue
Just plain old Western Truth.

Footnote — beret: French cap common in Montreal
chapeau: hat (FR.)
Molson: Canadian beer.
cravat: tie (FR.)

Nameless

U.S.S.R.

*The author traveled to Siberia, U.S.S.R.
in 1991.
The following are some of his observations.*

The Marxist Moan

Jesus founded his church
For his mighty Father above.
His ship sails at high speed
With no fear and much love.

Marx said, "We must start anew
Be rid of the church and steeple;
Let's stick to facts, Comrades
Religion is the opium of the people."

Now our ship is sinking
Marx made a mistake,
He did not gauge the addiction
Of our people's "drug" intake.

Magadan, Siberia

The Reds throttled many poets,
Banned the teachings of Moses and Christ.
Who needed poets and preachers?
Lenin was, "MR. KNOW IT ALL"
And Stalin was the, "ENLIGHTENMENT."

However, things are changing.
Glasnost has come and with it
People can say what they think.
The diehard Reds are losing out,
New ideas are taking over.

A Russian church is being built
And the "Good Book" is being read;
St. Vladimar's icons are back.
Stalin has been unmasked,
Lenin's image is tarnished.

The people have swallowed too much
Of the bread of adversity
And the waters of affliction.
Now is the time to sip the wine
Of freedom and democracy.

Here in this northern Siberian city
In a land of proud people
We see great natural resources
And an end to much suffering
This is Magadan.

Footnote — St. Vladimar: patron saint of the Russian church
Glasnost: openness
Gulags: the forced labor camps of Stalin
Pravda: the Russian newspaper, Pravda in English
is truth

Magadan, Siberia 1991

Greetings from Magadan city
On the Sea of Othotsk.
Here, East is really east.
The land is old, the city new,
It was built after Czar killing.

Our hotel was built in the 50s
It is not modern by our standards.
We can't take a hot shower,
The water system needs repairs.
When will it be fixed?

The time is early morning,
Buses are in the lot
Piling in the workers.
They appear to be "tag alongs"
Rather than lovers of the work.

The buildings look "prefab"
Are they beehives with
Workers or "drones" coming out?
Down the street is a farmer's market,
The closest thing to capitalism.

There is little toilet paper.
Newspapers become more useful.
There is a use for as well as truth in Pravda.
We brought our own roll of tissue.
Is toilet paper a capitalist luxury?

We see the usual northern dogs,
Not many, but they seem well fed.
Who knows? Maybe Stalin
Could feed some of his dogs
Better than most of his people?

Magadan, port of entry to the Gulags.
How much of the ground is enriched
By the dead killed by Stalin?
But soiled by his ghastly deeds?
We may never know the answer.

Sidewalks are hosed down each morning
By humans, not machines.
The grass is uncut beside the buildings,
There is no sight of lawn mowers.
Is there a shortage or don't they care?

The Red system is not working;
Our Siberian brothers know it.
Just remember they do not have
Six hundred years of the Magna Carta
Or the economics of Adam Smith.

Taiga, Tundra and Gold

It was a place of exile
With its bitter, bitter cold.
Truly, the end of the line
But with taiga, tundra and gold.

It was to this outback
Came the enemies of State
By the millions and more
At an ever increasing rate.

First it was a czarist prison
That had not seen the worst,
But this would come later
Under Stalin, the First.

Just a word or a whisper
Against the "Greatest of All"
Without judge or jury
Came the Siberia call

Now the prison has opened
The Reds "got the gate."
Winds of change are blowing
Seeds of freedom germinate.

The "Great Leader" is gone;
His statues come down with a thud.
The shining sea that he promised
Was only a puddle of mud.

Siberia is no longer a prison,
But still a rich, rich land.
From the Urals to the Strait
The people have a freer hand.

Neither is it a place of exile,
Red laws now are on hold.
Siberians will take charge
Of their tiaga, tundra and gold

Footnote— Tiaga: subarctic evergreen forests
Tundra: vast treeless arctic plains

Red History

"What is to be done?"
That is what Lenin said.
There were some replies,
"We'd rather be dead than Red,"
And they were.

Then came Gosplan and such
Under Stalin the First,
"Do it my way or be shot
Or die of hunger or thirst."
And many died.

Then came our Nikita
Who jarred the door.
The party did not like cracks
So he was dismissed as a boor.
A wiser clown?

Then came Comrade Breshnev
With his bugs of stagnation.
He drove us further down
The Road of Damnation.
So it went.

Next came some light
With Michael Sergevich,
"This is no joke Comrades
Our machine is in the ditch."
And it was.

Now we have President Yeltzin
Can he give us bread and threads?
Will he be able to repair
The wreck brought on by the Red?
Time will tell.

Footnote — Nikita: Nikita Khrushchev
Michael Sergevich : Gorbachev
Comrade Breshnev: Leonid Breshnev

New Saint

This is a plea for a change
In some old theology
To go along with the move
To new ideology.

We won't downgrade Mohamet
Nor take Christ off the cross.
We'll change only one Saint,
So for no one, a great loss.

We won't change names of saints
As from Crazy Horse to Holy Cow.
Our change will be a new St. Michael
Very much alive in Moscow.

It's the relics that must go
Or if you wish, call them "old bones."
Plus some ideas that are as outdated
As some of our old gramaphones.

We know that the new St. Michael
Won't promise Heaven or Holy Space,
But we would like some peace on earth
For the whole human race.

We know that we are taking a chance
Old saints died to be sainted.
Our new saint is still quite alive
And could wind up rather tainted.

Let's do away with the "old bones,"
and get down to "push and shove."
The newly robed St. Michael
Is Comrade M. Gorbachev.

In "The Church of What's Happening Now"

This was written at the height of President Gorbachev's (U.S.S.R.) popularity.

Pity on Them

A Verse on Russian refugees to the U.S.

Goodbye, that we must say
As we leave this Soviet city
Only here for one more day
Oh, what a great pity.

We leave "apparatchicks"
It was they who knew it all
Their game was politics
Soon for them a curtain call

They must walk the plank
For all their greed and gall
For it was they who shrank
From humanity's gentle call.

Yes, yes we are sad to say
We must leave this Soviet town
But we'll return some day
To pity those who put us down.

Why do we feel this way?
From us who felt the fetter?
To answer we must say,
"They didn't know any better."

The Jungle

There was no soggy ramp
Beside this jungle camp
To greet arriving planes
From long air lanes.

There was no jungle bush
But men with little push.
There were no slimy snakes
But lots of belly aches.

But there was some scurvy
In men, someways nervy;
Nearby some railroad track
Beside a station shack.

This jungle, just a space —
Some hobos' eating place.

Nameless

Tailings

Evita

I think of you, dear Evita
Here by the Plaza de Mayo
As I drink my margarita
Sad because you had to go.

I, poor descamisado
With nothing from early on
And no place but down to go
Till the coming of Peron.

Some said you were a whore
But you gave the "shirtless" bread
Clothes, comfort and a lot more
But now dear Leader you're dead.

We care not what you had been
Be it harlot or chaste
We saw you stick out your chin
For us of the "shirtless" caste.

Now you are gone dear Evita
I still have a few pesos
So, one more margarita
To us descamisados.

Oh, your spirit will live on
Though corpse cold as sturgeon
For us, you, Evita Peron
Did more than Mary, the Virgin.

Footnote — Evita: Eva Duarte Peron of Argentina, died July, 1952.
Descamisado: The poor working class of Argentina.
This verse is not an endorsement of Peronism nor is it critical of any
church, it is merely the feeling of descamisados and
others in Argentina at the time.
Plaza de Mayo: Main square in Buenos Aires

Legs, Legs, Legs

It was legs, legs, legs
Beneath the boiling sun;
it was down in Texas
That the work was done.

We may think of legs
As on a Broadway stage,
But here it was legs
In a universe of sage.

No rolling of a curtain
When the show began to play,
No plushy seats to sit on,
Just some Texas clay.

No staring at gold garters,
No fancy ushers for to tip,
Just a lot of noisy bragging
And the M.C.'s, "Let her rip!"

Oh the bulgy eyes
Blinking in the sun!
It was legs, legs, legs
Until the race was won.

Old Croaker won the race;
His hopping stood the test.
Cash rolled in for Swampy Joe,
The owner of the best.

It was legs, legs, legs
Out there in the west,
Not the legs on Broadway,
Just a frog jumping contest.

Beautiful but Cruel

It seems as quite natural
To call nature beautiful
But as a general rule
It is also very cruel.

Nature gives much to enchant
From great whale to tiny ant
And green mountains high and wide
But look at its other side.

See the birds, fish and mammal
All engaged in the scramble
Of fight for survival
Birth, death and revival.

Birds eat the fish that they catch
Fish eat the flies that they snatch
Wolves eat the deer that they chase
Boas eat what they embrace.

Man eats the moose that he slays
Ducks wind up as consommes
Gators nibble hogs and frogs
They wind up as gloves or clogs.

The end for all it is worth;
A grand meal for Mother Earth
Whom in gleeful mood devours;
Brings back as trees or flowers.

80

Nature's products — beautiful
Its methods, not merciful
Constant death and revival
A cruel fight for survival.

Old Vic's Ashes

Victoria is long gone
On to Kingdom Come
But part of her ashes
Are in the land of coke and rum.

She had help in spreading "Old Blighty"
From a bloody Brit named Disraeli.
If he lived in this day
He could be an Israeli.

The ashes we refer to
Are isles in the Carib Sea;
Portions of British pomp
What it is and used to be.

They are still with "John Bull"
By symbol of the Queen.
If Britain has any power
It is not to be seen.

Britain does not exert power
Except for the Queen's legality.
This part of Old Vic's ashes
Is tinctured with equality.

Yes Old Vic is long gone
Disraeli is no more,
But their actions still show
On the peaceful Caribbean shore.

Her body may be in St. Paul's
But the ashes of her power
Still clings to her people
At this late hour.

Footnote — Old Vic: Queen Victoria
Disraeli: her Prime Minister of Jewish background who
built the British Empire.
Old Blighty: Britain
John Bull: England
Ashes: The results of Victoria and Disraeli's building
and expanding the British Empire
St. Paul's: St. Paul's Church of England Cathedral

France in Manitoba

You need not go to Paris
Or the Cafe de la Paix.
Some of La Belle France
Is here on Manitoba clay.

E2 is our Sovereign Queen,
A symbol with no power at all.
French must be her spoken word
Just like it is in Montreal.

Here "Good Day" means "Bonjour,"
Maison is the word for home.
There is still some power
From the Vatican in Rome.

The city is dwarfed by Paris,
Its people much the same.
There is no McDonalds,
Chez Hamburger is the name.

There is no culture shock
You will need to face;
It is New France like the old,
But moving at a slower pace.

*When the British gained control of Canada they granted Quebec the
right to keep their Roman (catholic) religion and the French
language. However, due to immigration we see what might be called
"Little Quebecs" especially in the prairie provinces in Western
Canada. This verse refers to a Little Quebec in Manitoba.*

Before and After

He said, " I'll climb the highest mountain,
I'll swim the widest sea,
And cross the broadest desert,
If you will marry me."

She cried, "No sooner said than done!"
So to the preacher off they go,
And next to stand the litmus test
Would it be happiness or woe?

He climbed the highest mountain,
He swam the widest sea,
He trudged the broadest desert,
But, oh, surprised was he

When forty miles from Cairo
Came a letter postmarked, Nome,
"I am filing for divorce;
Can't stand a man who's never home."

Man and Moth
or Nuclear Folly

Let's think of the moth that we see
In his flight straight in to the flame.
How mad, mad can this insect be?
But really, no madder than we.

We may have the same cremation
Of humankind, just like the moth,
In a nuclear conflagration
Even blest by men of the cloth.

The act of the moth we forgive
Because he is blinded by light,
But why can't man be objective?
Fact is, we can't see wrong from right.

We dismiss the moth with, "He's mad."
As he flys to instant suicide.
His end, it is certainly sad,
But no suicide plus homicide.

Man has gone to the moon.
Yet, he is as blind as the moth,
Using discovery that may soon
Fit any survivors for sack cloth

And condemn them to an end
In the ashes with no more to come.
Oh Allah, oh God, oh my friend,
How smart can we be, still so dumb.

The Ticket

They went halfsies on the home
She would get a monthly check
And could keep her motor car
That was more than just a wreck.

All the bills were his to pay;
She had money in the bank —
He took it as just fickle fate
With no God to blame or thank.

He signed all the legal forms,
Crossed all the important Ts,
Bought her a ticket on Pan Am
And threw in some togs and skis.

We agree that he acted
As a real gentlemen will.
Why the need for such a ticket
To rake the high leaving bill?

When we asked, came this reply,
"Glad you opened up your mouth
It's a one-way to the Faulklands
I hope that she likes the South.

"I must settle with decorum;
She requires a vacation.
Why should I quibble on a ticket
To a faraway location?"

Something is Missing
(Montreal - 1992)

Two full beers on the table,
The time is still before eight.
This is a better pub
Opening early, closing late.

The old timer across from us
Begins to lap his beer up.
Two girls in the corner,
Beer for them too — "Bottoms up."

The girls puff on their cigs
This is not the Baptist church
For them, such things as prayer
Have been left in the lurch.

Here we are on Stanley street
In the great city of Montreal
The scene is not new except that
No Americans are here for a "ball."

Not new is what we said
True as to scene, not the air
The speech coming over its waves
Is all French with no English there.

We are not culture vultures
And our French is in order,
But the "missing something" keeps
Yankee money within the U.S. border.

Commentary on the effect of the suppression of the English language in the province of Quebec and the loss of tourist trade from Americans who do not speak French.

The End of Ethics

In Yukon, a maid so sweet
Waits up there, my mate to be.
She's half Chip and Innuit
Another mongrel, just like me.

My daddy came up from Rio
"Blueblood" there brings on a laugh.
Mom was born in Point Barrow
So, I too am half and half.

Yukon Flo and I will wed
And when comes conception day
It can be with gusto said,
"One more mongrel on the way."

Is that not for most, their lot?
With ethnics and race passe,
All stew in the melting pot
Here in our world of today.

Footnote — Chip: Chippewayan Indian
Innuit: Native word for Eskimo
Mongrel: Used here to denote mixture with no
derogatory connotation.

A Toast

Our life is a flicker,
Just one little sizzle
Smallest beyond imagination
In the space of time
Allotted us here.

Let's have no delusions,
Just think of the millions
Who came and may come later.
We are just the tiniest cog
In the largest machine.

Insignificant creature,
Like the smallest fish
In the largest ocean
At the complete mercy
Of the Sea of Time.

This is the way
Of our lives.
One little flicker
And then again
Darkness for us.

So, here is a toast
To making the most
Of that little flicker
Or space of time
That we call our lives.

Gathered Along the Way

When there is an opportunity to do good, let us do it. Let us resist saying or doing things that will harm ourselves or others, for it is unknown when comes the termination of our human association when apology or retraction will be unattainable forever.
Our primary duty in living is to be as happy as possible and in turn make the people around us the same.
— Eskimo Philosophy

The three hardest things to do are to return love for hate, say, "I was wrong," and include the excluded.

A calm voice governs.— Toastmaster Training

Most friction between people
is caused by the tone of voice.

To those who feel, life is a tragedy;
To those who think, life is a comedy.

Temper is what gets us into trouble,
pride is what keeps us there.

Our past is a bucket of ashes.

Sail, don't drift.

Rebuffs are merely rungs in the ladder of success.
— Robert W. Service

Never wrestle with a pig.
You both get dirty and the pig loves it.

The exalted shall be humbled and the humble shall be exalted.— The Bible

The North has got him. — A Yukonism

Breakup

Like a roar of thunder
The ice breaks asunder,
From Tagish Lake to Bering Sea
By highest mountain, past shortest tree.

Tearing, gnawing, splashing
As an invisible knife slashing.
Ice and water rushes on and on
From dawn to dusk to dawn.

Before, a solid rock
Of ice, like rock;
Now just chunk of cold
Since spring has taken hold.

Yes, ice is rushing on
Breaking has come to the Yukon.

An Inuk Speaks

The skyline of Toronto
Is something to look on to;
Others say to have a ball,
"Go southeast to Montreal."

No, we do not have the urge
For such money to splurge
In some other unknown place
We'll just stick to empty space.

We feel of serenity
Up here by the Beaufort Sea
Where it is colder than cold.
Nature has us in its hold.

Keep your bloody city hassle
Let us keep our icy castle
And stay by this Arctic Sea
From here to Eternity.

Footnote — Inuk: See below

On April 1st, 1999 Canada gained a new territory — Nunavut. It was formerly part of the Northwest Territories. Nunuvat is composed of 1.9 million square kilometers and spans three time zones. It's population, overwhelmingly Innuit, is only in the thousands. In the past the natives were called Eskimos, an uncomplimentary Cree term which means, "eaters of raw meat." The correct term in the plural is Innuit and one person is called Inuk. Innuit seems to be able to be translated as, "the people." It seems that the origin of the Innuit is from Asia and, about 5,000 years ago, they immigrated across the then existent Bering Land Bridge. They moved into the eastern and central arctic from the north coast of Alaska about 1,000 years ago.

The Further Apart

The further apart
The closer we get
Some months to go
Quite a way yet

It must look real
You be the louse
Me in the Big Apple
You — the White House.

The further apart
The closer we get
Make the yokels believe
Old hat — no sweat.

We're a foxy duet
Both the same goal
You have your "birds"
I'll play the hurt role

The further apart
The closer we get
Let's fool them again
Senator ME — a good bet.

It's all deja vu.
Experts in phony?
They'll gobble it up
They love our baloney

The further apart
The closer we get
Keep your distance
No senate seat yet.

Nameless

To order additional copies of

Nameless

or receive a copy of the complete
Savage Press catalog

Contact us at:

Phone Orders: 1-800-732-3867

Voice and Fax: (715) 394-9513

e-mail: savpress@spacestar.com

Visit online at: savpress.com

Visa or MasterCard accepted

PRESS

Box 115, Superior, WI 54880 (715) 394-9513